Copyright © 1987, 1996 by Empak Publishing Company

ISBN 0-922162-4-2 (Volume IV)
ISBN 0-922162-15-8 (Volume Set)

A Salute to Black Civil Rights Leaders

EMPAK PUBLISHING COMPANY

Publisher & Editor: Richard L. Green
Assoc. Editor: Dorothy M. Love-Carroll, Roger G. Fuelster
Researcher: Ted Evans
Production: Dickinson & Associates, Inc.
Illustration: S. Gaston Dodson
Preface: Richard L. Green

PREFACE

Borrowing on Frederick Douglass' infinite wisdom, "Without a struggle, there can be no progress," it is also factual that without the knowledge of one's own history, there can be no appreciable future. Worldwide, noted educators and sociologists are in accord that the suppression of Black history has been a deliberate denial and major impediment to the enrichment and progress of Black America.

To stem the tide of Black-on-Black crime, the erosion of the Black family structure, the frustration and low self-esteem within our ranks, we, as concerned Black Americans, employing our heritage and struggle, must reach back and teach our Black youth (at an early age) that they, as a race of people, have a reason to be proud. That in spite of prevailing discriminatory obstacles, with determination, they, too, can aspire and achieve.

Although the previous three volumes *Historic Black Women; Scientists & Inventors; and Pioneers*, produced by Empak Publishing Company, contained many profiles of notable and historic civil rights activists, a special direction has been taken with our fourth booklet, *A Salute to Black Civil Rights Leaders,* which specifically illustrates the various fronts on which civil rights have been fought. The nineteen historic Black Americans whose contributions are highlighted in this volume fought in the trenches of racism for human rights and decency to ensure the furtherance of Black America and all mankind.

Focusing on various historical periods and subject matters, plus fulfilling an existing void, Empak's primary objective has been to present Black history in an *inspiring, concise* and *affordable* manner, thus allowing maximum penetration and appeal to the masses of Black Americans—from the young to the old—in all walks of life. In so doing, we have attempted to: (1) raise the consciousness of Black America, (2) instill a knowledge and respect of one's own history, (3) establish a sense of ethnic pride and self esteem, and (4) provide a cohesiveness, through the positive teachings of Black History, which will spur Black America to the reality and wisdom of self-determination, the objective pooling of spiritual, political and economical energies and resources.

We, at Empak, envision that our present and future publications will be instrumental in expanding the horizon and interest of Black history throughout all segments of society. We're optimistic that our Black history booklets will provide a stimulus and quest for additional in-depth study of the exciting, historic Black Americans presented within our series.

Richard L. Green, President
Empak Publishing Company

CONTENTS

BIOGRAPHIES:

Editor's Note: Due to this booklet's space limitations, some facets on the lives of the above noted Civil Rights Leaders have been omitted.

DAISY GATSON BATES
1922-

Bates and the "Little Rock Nine" received national attention in 1957, when an attempt was made to place nine Black children in the all-White Central High School in Little Rock, Arkansas. In a two year struggle, she was considered the moving force behind Little Rock's integration efforts.

Born in 1922, in Huttig, Arkansas, Daisy later became the adopted daughter of Mr. and Mrs. Orles Gatson. After graduating from high school, Daisy attended Philander Smith and Shorter colleges in Little Rock. At age eight, she learned, through a playmate, that the Gatsons were not her real parents, for she had lost her mother through an act of mob violence. Late one afternoon, her mother was taken from her home by three White men. Her body was found the next day in a local pond; she had been raped. This proved to be too much for Daisy's father who placed her in the Gatson's care.

In 1941, Daisy married L.C. Bates, a journalist, and together they started a newspaper, the *Arkansas State Press,* in Little Rock. They then launched an all-out campaign against all forms of injustices perpetrated against Blacks. In the early months of the newspaper, circulation reached ten thousand and the Bates became a strong force in championing the rights of Blacks.

In 1942, Daisy covered a story involving the coldblooded murder of a Black soldier by a city policeman. She reported that the killing was "one of the most bestial murders in the annals of Little Rock." She went on to say that after the officer had thrown the soldier to the ground, he pumped five bullets into his prostrate body.

A few days after Daisy ran the story, she lost a substantial amount of advertising from White stores. The future of the paper seemed grim, but the Bates began working 18 hours a day; once again circulation rose, reaching 20,000. They expanded their efforts to include better housing conditions, jobs, and courtroom representation for Blacks.

When the famous *Brown vs. Board of Education* case in 1954, resulted in a Supreme Court decision that segregation in public schools was unconstitutional, Daisy Bates took the national spotlight as a promoter in desegregating Central High in Little Rock, Arkansas. Integration in many Arkansas schools was carried out without incident or violence until Orval Faubus became governor in 1955.

Of the seventeen Black students selected for enrollment by Daisy Bates and the NAACP, and screened by the school board, eight withdrew out of fear. When the remaining nine children attempted to enter the White school, National Guardsmen barred the entrance at Faubus' orders. The children were not allowed to enter the school until President Eisenhower sent the 101st Airborne Division to escort them.

Because of Daisy's involvement, rocks were thrown through her windows and crosses burned on her lawn. After the loss of thousands of dollars in advertising revenue, the *State Press* was forced out of operation. Nightly, her home had to be protected by armed guards.

After the Little Rock incident, Daisy continued her fight for equal rights. She spoke at the Civil Rights March on Washington in 1963, pledging to stop fighting only when Black Americans could sit, walk, kneel and study in any public place in this country. In recognition for her outstanding efforts, she received awards, citations and honorary degrees from more than forty organizations.

Daisy Bates was awarded "Woman of the Year" twice, "Outstanding Citizen of the Year for 1957," "One of the Top Nine News Personalities of the World for 1957," was listed in *Who's Who in American Women*, and was the recipient of the NAACP Spingarn Medal.

GEORGE THOMAS DOWNING
1819-1903

George T. Downing was a successful businessman, a persuasive civil rights leader in the struggle for fair and equal justice for Black troops during the Civil War, and a crusader for equality in educational privileges for Black youths.

The eldest son of Thomas and Rebecca Downing, George was born in New York City on December 30, 1819. During his early school years, Downing and other Black children were the target of insulting jeers and stones from Whites. Black parents had to accompany their children to and from school to ensure their safety. Young Downing refused parental escort. When the need arose, he boldly organized a group of Black boys to counteract the hostile White crowds.

Even as a young man, Downing realized the plight of Blacks and exhibited an unflinching stance. At fourteen, he formed a literary society to discuss issues pertaining to the Black cause. The group decided to stop celebrating the Fourth of July because "the Declaration of Independence was to Black America a perfect mockery." Downing attended Hamilton College in Oneida County, New York, and later married Serena Leanora DeGrasse, the daughter of a wealthy landowner.

Before reaching adulthood, Downing became an active agent on the Underground Railroad. Once, he was arrested for breaking a fugitive slave out of a New York jail. In 1854, he pulled a daring act of bravery which could have cost him his life. When city policemen attacked a group of Black demonstrators and took their freedom banner, Downing, overpowered with rage, rushed into the mob of police, retrieved the torn banner and returned it to the marchers amidst expressions of awe and admiration.

Downing never failed to strike a blow for the freedom of his people. He expressed his views on Black concerns in all areas. While residing in Rhode Island, he fought laboriously for twelve years (1857-1869) to establish integration in federally-supported schools. He helped to repeal a law requiring Blacks to own $250 worth of property to be eligible to vote; he also fought a similar law affecting Irish immigrants.

Downing is credited with the abolition of a nine o'clock curfew for Blacks, and the passage of the public accommodations law in Washington, D.C. As an enlisted man in the Civil War, he personally spoke to the governor to ensure that Black and White troops were treated the same.

While unselfishly fighting for the rights of others, Downing also achieved personal status and wealth. He established a successful catering business in 1850, and built the swanky Sea Girt Hotel in 1854. He suffered a financial loss of over $40,000 when the hotel was destroyed by fire in 1860. However by 1888, Downing was able to acquire substantial real estate in Rhode Island. He constructed a building on Downing Block and rented a portion to the federal government for a Naval Academy hospital.

For over a decade, Downing managed a restaurant in the House of Representatives in the Nation's capitol. It was known that Mr. Downing openly refused to adhere to a "color line." His policy was to serve Whites and Blacks alike, and would advise his head waiter to "send to me anyone who may complain."

On July 21, 1903, George T. Downing died after a long illness, survived by his six children, a brother and a nephew. As stated in the *Boston Globe*, "His skin fades almost out of sight when it is remembered that he fought not only for his own race, but that his purse were always open in helping all races who were oppressed."

■ DR. WILLIAM EDWARD BURGHARDT DUBOIS ■
1868-1963

An educator, historian, sociologist, philosopher, civil rights leader, and apostle of peace, W.E.B. DuBois was one of America's most brilliant scholars. DuBois was a professor of Greek, Latin, German, English, economics and history. He authored well over 100 books, articles and poems, and edited publications on virtually every aspect of the Afro-American culture.

Dr. DuBois, born February 23, 1868 in Great Barrington, Mass., was the only child of Alfred and Mary Silvina DuBois. From early childhood, he exhibited remarkable intellectual brilliance and was the only Black student to graduate from Great Barrington High in 1884. In 1888, he received a B.A. from Fisk University. In 1890, he earned another B.A., cum laude, from Harvard University, and also an M.A. in 1891. He received a Ph.D. in 1895, becoming the first Black American to earn this degree from Harvard. In 1896, DuBois married Nina Gomer and they later had two children.

DuBois introduced his first works of importance, *The Suppression of the African Slave Trade* and *The Philadelphia Negro* in 1896. The former was 335 pages and required voluminous research which he supported with abundant footnotes, lengthy appendices, and a fifteen page bibliography. It became an indispensable source for the study of the era, 1638 to 1870, of "man's inhumanity to man." The latter was the first study of scientific importance by a Black American on the social conditions affecting Blacks.

DuBois was acclaimed a great American essayist after he authored *The Souls of Black Folk* in 1903. It became a classic of the times and was widely quoted. His scholarly works adhered to his ideas of "seeking the truth on the pure assumption that it is worth seeking."

Dr. DuBois, a fierce antagonist against racial injustice, was a great leader of protest and was called "An Authentic African Radical." He founded the Niagara Movement in 1905, which later became the NAACP. His movement advocated immediate full-citizenship rights for Blacks. At its second meeting in 1906, DuBois declared, "We will not be satisfied to take one jot less than our full manhood rights. We claim for ourselves every single right that belongs to a freeborn American ... and until we get these rights we will never cease to protest and assail the ears of America."

In 1919, Dr. DuBois fathered the Pan-African Congress, in Paris, to focus world opinion on the problems of Black people everywhere. He urged the British to give governmental rights to Black colonies of Africa and the West Indies. Over the years, he became one of the most controversial Black leaders in the U.S.

During the 1950s, he was the leader of the World Peace Information Center which led to his indictment as an unregistered foreign agent. DuBois wrote, "it is a curious thing that I am called upon to defend myself against charges for openly advocating one thing all people want—peace." Two million signatures were collected in his behalf before he took the stand, and the case was dismissed.

Dr. W.E.B. DuBois died on August 27, 1963, after becoming a citizen of Ghana, Africa. Although no predominantly White American universities saw fit to award him any honorary degrees, he received more than his share from other noted universities in this country and abroad. In 1969, Great Barrington reluctantly authorized a memorial park surrounding the DuBois family home.

With truth, intellect and the vigor of his pen, Dr. W.E.B. DuBois' entire life was spent trying to unbind the enslaving shackles of racism and prejudice the world over.

JAMES LEONARD FARMER
1920-

James Farmer co-founder and national director of the Congress of Racial Equality (CORE), was also Assistant Secretary of the Department of Health, Education and Welfare (HEW), program director of the NAACP, and organizer of several unions.

James was born on January 12, 1920, in Marshall, Texas. He was one of the three Farmer children. His father, a professor at Wiley College in Marshall, held the distinction of being the first Black in Texas to hold a Ph.D. degree, which he obtained from Boston University. Farmer attended public schools in the South and, in 1938, at the age of eighteen, he graduated from Wiley with a B.S. degree in chemistry.

In 1941, Farmer received a Bachelor of Divinity degree from Howard University. However, he refused to be ordained, since the Methodist Churches in the South were segregated. Farmer stated, "I didn't see how I could honestly preach the Gospel of Christ in a Church that practiced discrimination."

Farmer later became a race relations secretary for the Fellowship of Reconciliation, a Christian pacifist group, serving until 1945. It was while in this post that he helped form the Congress of Racial Equality. CORE started as a local chapter in Chicago, in 1942, and branched into a national organization in 1943. CORE was an integrated organization that employed the Gandhian principle of nonviolent action against racial segregation and discrimination in the United States. Its main objective and focus was to eradicate de facto school segregation, obtain equality in jobs and housing, and eliminate police brutality.

While maintaining his ties with CORE, Farmer worked as an organizer for several unions and served as a program director for the NAACP. Farmer was CORE's first national chairman, and became its national director on February 1,

1961. Under his leadership, CORE successfully employed the direct tactics of "Freedom Rides," sit-ins, stand-ins, sleep-ins, eat-ins, and jail-ins to achieve its goals.

On March 13, 1961 Farmer directed a "Freedom Ride" through the South to challenge segregation of interstate bus terminals. In May 1963, he went to North Carolina to lead demonstrations and coordinate protest movements in Greensboro, Durham, and High Point. In August of 1963, he went to Plaquemines, Louisiana to lead a civil rights march and was imprisoned. And, as a result, Farmer was unable to take part in the "March on Washington" on August 28th, an historic event in which he was co-chairman.

In April 1964, demonstrating against the condition of Blacks in New York City, CORE initiated a protest against the New York's World Fair. In January 1965, CORE aided in the desegregation of Bogalusa, Louisiana. In July 1965, CORE adopted a resolution calling for the withdrawal of U.S. troops from Vietnam. Not only did Farmer creatively plan most of CORE's activities, he also participated in them, and was jailed many times.

To pursue other Black liberation programs, Farmer stepped down as CORE's national director in early 1966, and was succeeded by Floyd B. McKissick. In July 1966, he was named a consultant to New Jersey's anti-poverty program, and he joined the faculty of Lincoln University, as a professor of social welfare, in September.

Appointed by President Nixon, Farmer was confirmed by the Senate in March 1969, as Assistant Secretary of Health, Education, and Welfare (HEW) with special emphasis on the Black youth of America. Farmer resigned from HEW on December 7, 1970, stating, "ponderous bureaucracy prevented me from achieving gains sufficient or fast enough to satisfy my appetite for progress."

Throughout his struggle for civil rights, Farmer has gained the respect and recognition of being a tough and audacious leader. Although James Farmer, married and the father of two daughters, terminated his government employment, he did not relinquish his fight for his people.

MARCUS M. GARVEY
1887-1940

Marcus Mosiah Garvey, a compelling orator, organizer and Black nationalist, advocated economic independence and Black internationalism as an answer to the Black man's plight.

Marcus was born on August 17, 1887 in St. Ann's Bay, Jamaica, the youngest of eleven children of Marcus and Sarah Garvey. Both parents were of pure African lineage, giving Garvey a strong sense of racial pride.

Having to quit school at the age of fourteen, Garvey went to work as a printer's apprentice in Kingston, Jamaica. Since he was highly intelligent and an avid reader, gifted in the use of language, his newspaper training was to become an important factor in his later years. Garvey also became impressed with the power of oratory persuasion and spent hours in his room reciting and learning new words from a small dictionary he carried.

Concerned about the injustices perpetrated against his race, in 1910, Garvey went to Central and South America in search of better opportunities. However, in every city and every country, Garvey was sickened by the exploitation of his people. He later went to London and briefly studied at Birkbeck College, where he met Africans for the first time. An Egyptian nationalist inspired Garvey's interest in Africa's independence and gave him the opportunity to write for his *Africa Times and Orient Review*. He came upon a copy of Booker T. Washington's autobiography, *Up from Slavery*, and was moved by his philosophy of Black self-help.

In 1914, armed with a determination to help his people, Garvey returned to Jamaica and founded the Universal Negro Improvement Association (UNIA). The UNIA's goals were to promote racial unity through education, encourage racial pride, establish worldwide commercial activity, and develop

Africa. The UNIA's first project was the establishment of a trades school, patterned after Tuskegee Institute, however it failed to materialize and Garvey sought help from the United States, at the invitation of Booker T. Washington. Unfortunately, Washington died prior to Garvey's arrival.

Within two months, after arriving in New York on March 23, 1916, Garvey had recruited nearly 2,000 members in the UNIA. He traveled throughout the 38 states, preaching racial pride and independence. Within a five year span, he had recruited more than a million members. There were 700 branches in the States and more than 200 branches in the West Indies, Central America and northern South America. In January 1918, to catapult his ideas worldwide, he began publishing the *Negro World,* which became a leading weekly newspaper.

In 1919, Garvey started the Black Star Ship Line, consisting of the *Yarmouth, Shadyside* and *Kanawha* fleet. His Negro Factories Corporation provided loans and technical assistance to Blacks developing their own companies. Selling stock to Blacks at $5.00 a share, a chain of cooperative businesses was also established. However, his UNIA ventures soon fell upon financial hardship. And, despite his efforts to reorganize, he was arrested in 1922, and unjustly charged with mail fraud in promoting the sale of stock in the Black Star Ship Line. After years of appeal and the support of many friends, he began serving his sentence in 1925. In 1927, his five year sentence was commuted and he was ordered deported to Jamaica by President Coolidge.

In 1940, Marcus Garvey died in London at the age of fifty-two, survived by his second wife, Amy Jacques Garvey, and two sons, Marcus Jr. and Junius. Garvey stirred the imagination of Black Americans, and he created in them an intense interest in their culture, history, achievements, and future. His legacy is simply stated, "Up' You mighty race, You can accomplish what you will."

FRANCIS JAMES GRIMKE
1850-1937

Francis J. Grimke, author, student of law, and an outspoken scholarly minister, used his church as a battleground. His scathing sermons were weapons in defending the rights of Blacks.

Born in Charleston, South Carolina on November 4, 1850, Francis was the second of three sons of Henry Grimke, a White plantation slaveholder, and Nancy Weston, a slave servant of the household. Francis' father died in 1852, leaving the family in hands of the eldest son, Montague.

When young Francis reached the age of ten, having previously lived as a de facto free person, his White half-brother tried to enslave him. He escaped and joined the army, serving as a valet to a Confederate officer, but after two years was found again by Montague and placed in a Charleston workhouse. Francis became ill and almost died from exposure and bad treatment. He was allowed to return to his mother, but before he was able to regain his strength and flee his mother's house, Montague sold him, and he was forced to work as a servant until the end of the Civil War.

After he was freed, Mrs. P. Pillsbury, a White abolitionist, arranged for Grimke to enter Lincoln University in Pennsylvania, and he received moral and financial support from his White "aunt." Francis was a superior student, graduating, in 1870, with high honors and later studying law at Lincoln and Howard Universities. In 1875, he entered the ministry at Princeton Theological Seminary, graduated in 1878, and immediately accepted a pastorship in Washington, D.C. He later married the well-known Charlotte Forten, who died in 1914. Their only child, Theodora Cornelia, was born and died in 1880.

Rev. Grimke, thrust into the role of social prophet, condemned the hypocrisy of American life as well as that of the

Church. The American Bible Society, noted evangelists, and his own denomination became targets of his criticisms. He circulated numerous sermons, *God and the Race Problem,* and *Jim Crow Christianity and the Negro,* and delivered many lectures in an effort to expose the growing segregation movement in the Christian churches.

As chairman of the Committee of Religion and Ethics of the Afro-Presbyterian Council, Grimke's position gave him a platform to develop and strengthen its character of moral excellence and to achieve social and spiritual salvation. Although Grimke considered himself to be a radical and an agitator, he shaped his ministry to conform to his perception of the pastor as moral exemplar. However, when lynching and race riots broke out in southern states, he became enraged. He stated that it was the duty of Blacks to be prepared to defend themselves against organized, murderous assaults. After the Springfield, Illinois race riots in 1908, Grimke joined other concerned Black and White leaders in forming the NAACP.

Rev. Grimke gave financial support and gifts to Howard and Lincoln Universities to help Black youths attain a higher education. He owned an impressive library consisting of over one thousand volumes of selected works on literature, theology, philosophy, history, art and other subjects. When he retired in 1925, he divided his books between Lincoln and Howard, where they were commissioned as the Francis J. Grimke Collections. He also gave $4,000 to Lincoln and $4,500 to the Board of Pensions of the Presbyterian Church in America.

Prior to his death in 1937, Francis J. Grimke stated, "the Federation of White Churches, consciously or unconsciously, stands for a Christianity that lays greater emphasis upon the color of a man's skin than upon his Christian character."

Fannie Lou Hamer was the founder and vice-chairwoman of the Mississippi Freedom Democratic Party (MFDP), which was successful in unseating the all-White Democratic Party in 1968. She earned the sobriquet "First Lady of Civil Rights."

Fannie was born on October 6, 1917, in Ruleville, Mississippi, the last of twenty children of Jim and Lou Ella Townsend. Her parents were sharecroppers and although the family picked from fifty to sixty bales of cotton yearly, they had very little to eat and were often without shoes.

Fannie went to school periodically until she reached the sixth grade. At age twenty-four, she married Perry Hamer, a tractor driver, and moved with him to Sunflower County, near Ruleville, and they became sharecroppers. Realizing that they could not have children, they adopted two daughters who eventually provided them with grandchildren.

In 1962, Fannie Lou became involved with the civil rights movement when the Southern Christian Leadership Conference and the Student Nonviolent Co-ordinating Committee held a meeting in Ruleville. She and seventeen others agreed to go to the county courthouse and attempt to register to vote. They were asked twenty-one questions, one of which was to copy and interpret a part of the Mississippi Constitution. They all failed. Fannie Lou left a warning that she would be back again and again until she passed.

On the way home, the driver of their bus was stopped by the police and was fined $100 for driving a bus "of the wrong color." When she reached home, her employer advised her that "we are not ready for this in Mississippi." "I didn't register for you," Fannie said, "I tried to register for me." She and her family were forced to leave their home, and the employer took their furnishings and their car.

Fannie Lou's life became a living hell. She was hunted like a dog, shot at, cursed and abused by angry mobs of White men. On January 10, 1963, Fannie Lou passed her voter registration test. Returning home, she was arrested by policemen who told her "we are going to make you wish you were dead." "They ordered two Black prisoners to beat me until they were exhausted, my body was hard, and seemed dead...I got this blood clot in my left eye—the sight's nearly gone .... And my kidney was injured from the blows given to my back," Fannie Lou recalled. She later heard the officers plotting to kill her. Word of her mistreatment reached Dr. King, who demanded her immediate release. Fannie Lou and her friends were carried out of jail, bloody, bruised, and unconscious, by Andrew Young and James Bevel. Fannie refused to let this horrid, brutal experience deter her.

In 1964, Fannie Lou, an articulate and forceful speaker, became the first Black woman to run for Congress from the Second District of Mississippi. The name of the MFDP was eventually changed to the Mississippi Loyalist Democratic Party and, in 1968, the credentials committee granted the MLDP its rightful seat at the National Democratic Convention held in Chicago. Fannie Lou received a standing ovation as she took her seat, and subsequently received speaking invitations from across the nation.

In 1970, Fannie received the first of several honorary doctorate degrees. Over time, she received many awards and citations. Realizing a life-long dream, Fannie L. Hamer raised over one million dollars for Sunflower County, and she also established a 680 acre complex (Freedom Farmer Cooperative) to house and feed the poor of all races. She later founded the Fannie Lou Hamer Day Care Center for the children of working mothers.

Fannie Lou Hamer died on March 14, 1977. The State of Mississippi passed a resolution praising and commending her life and her struggle for human dignity.

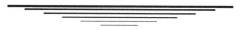

DR. GEORGE EDMUND HAYNES
1880-1960

George E. Haynes, Ph.D., a noted sociologist and founder of the National Urban League, devoted his life to the betterment of Blacks through the establishment of socioeconomic programs.

George Haynes was born in Pine Bluff, Arkansas in 1880, the eldest of two children of Louis and Mattie Haynes. He and his sister attended segregated public schools in Pine Bluff. Haynes graduated from Fisk University in 1903 and received an M.A. from Yale University in 1904. He maintained an excellent academic record. Haynes was awarded a scholarship to study at Yale's Divinity College.

Helping to support his widowed mother and younger sister, he worked as a traveling student adviser for the International Committee of the YMCA, visiting southern Black colleges. Haynes provided young college men with moral and spiritual leadership, encouraging a commitment to the betterment of social and economic conditions of Blacks.

During 1906 and 1907, Haynes attended summer sessions at the University of Chicago, studying economics and sociology. He became the first Black to graduate from the New York School of Social Work, at Columbia University, in 1910, and in 1912, he was the first Black to receive a Ph.D. in economics from Columbia. His doctoral dissertation, entitled *The Negro At Work In New York City*, was publishied in 1912. Haynes married Elizabeth Ross during this period and had one son.

When Black migration to northern cities was of paramount concern to sociologists, Haynes sought to help Blacks make a smooth transition from their rural environment to city life. He became involved with the Association for the Protection of Colored Women in 1905, and later with the Committee for Improving the Industrial Conditions of Negroes in New York. Haynes subsequently created the Committee on Urban Conditions among Negroes in 1910, and out of this committee sprang the National Urban League. Haynes wrote scholarly studies in conjunction with these committees, and trained Black social workers at Fisk. The National Urban League expanded rapidly.

In 1917, Haynes transferred the leadership of the League to Eugene K. Jones, and moved into a post with the U.S. Department of Labor as director of Black economics. He was later given a membership on the President's Unemployment Conference. In 1921, he became an organizer and one of the first executive secretaries of the Department of Race Relations of the Federal Council of the Churches of Christ in America. He served in this position until 1947. He conducted surveys on the work of the YMCA and proposed programs for African countries. He achieved national prominence and, from 1948 to 1955, he served as a consultant on Africa to the World Committee of the YMCA.

Dr. George Haynes was a member of the commission to study the need for a State University in New York, and later served on its board of trustees after it was established in 1948. He taught in New York's city colleges for nearly ten years. He authored *The Negro At Work During The World War,* and twice co-authored the article on the *American Negro* in the *Encyclopedia Britannica.*

After his first wife's death in 1953, he married Olyve Love Jeter in 1955. Following his death in 1960, his wife preserved his manuscripts, established the George Edmund Haynes Collection at Yale University and donated other significant writings to Fisk University.

REV. JESSE LOUIS JACKSON
1941-

By a consensus of the polls in 1983, the Rev. Jesse Louis Jackson, a Baptist minister, was named the most important Black leader in America. In 1984, he earned a permanent place in the history of this nation when he became a major candidate and forcefully ran for the presidency of the United States.

Jackson was born on October 8, 1941, in Greenville, South Carolina. In 1943, his mother, Helen Burns, married Charles Henry Jackson, who adopted Jesse and raised him as his own. In 1959, Jesse graduated from Sterling High. For racial reasons, he turned down a contract to play baseball for the Chicago White Sox, instead, accepted a football scholarship from the University of Illinois. When the coach informed him that Blacks could never be star quarterbacks, Jesse left Illinois and entered North Carolina Agricultural & Technical State University. There, he starred on the football team, and was soon to become a raging force in the civil rights movement.

In 1963, Jesse became a leader in the student sit-in campaign to integrate public facilities in Greensboro, North Carolina. After earning a B.S. degree in sociology at A&T in 1964, he worked for the Congress of Racial Equality. He entered the Chicago Theological Seminary, but quit after two years to work with Dr. Martin Luther King, Jr. and was later ordained in 1968. King appointed him Chicago Director of the Southern Christian Leadership Conference's Operation Breadbasket, established, in 1962, to negotiate with White-owned corporations to hire Blacks, since, according to SCLC's rationale, Blacks were major contributors to the economy of the nation.

In 1966, Jackson initiated a series of boycotts. When his demands upon White business were not met, Blacks were advised to withdraw their patronage. News of Jackson's resounding success through Operation Breadbasket soon spread across the nation.

After Dr. Martin Luther King, Jr.'s assassination in 1968, Rev. Jackson remained with the SCLC and executed Kings plan for a Poor Peoples Campaign. In 1969, he produced Chicago's first Black Exposition. In 1971, he severed his association with SCLC and founded Operation PUSH (People United to Serve Humanity), which promotes economic independence along with self-worth.

Worldwide, the Rev. Jesse Jackson has had a major influence on numerous political and humanitarian issues. He was responsible for the liberation of a Black Navy pilot, Lt . Robert Goodman, Jr. from a Middle East prison. Also, the families of the American hostages in Lebanon. President Aquino of the Philippines, and other heads of state have sought his counsel.

As an outgrowth of his 1984 presidential campaign, Jackson established a national office for his Rainbow Coalition in Washington, D.C. The primary goal of the Rainbow Coalition is to unite and weld the poor and disenfranchised of all races into a strong political force.

Rev. Jesse Jackson, addressing major issues affecting Blacks in this nation and abroad, coupled with his ability to command audiences with key policy makers, gives meaning and breadth to two of his significant credos ... "I am somebody" and "Nobody will save us from us for us but us." Dubbed the "country preacher," Jesse Jackson is a persuasive orator and an audacious fighter for equal rights for Blacks and other minorities.

DR. MARTIN LUTHER KING, JR.
1929-1968

Dr. Martin Luther King, Jr., a southern Baptist minister, author, and undoubtedly one of the most effective civil rights leaders in this nation's history, preached universal love and brotherhood, and led nonviolent demonstrations and sit-ins all over the country for racial equality.

Martin Luther King, Jr. was born on January 15, 1929 in Atlanta, Georgia, the middle child of Rev. Martin Luther, Sr. and Alberta King. As a young man, King had an insatiable thirst for knowledge. Throughout his academic career, he maintained an exceptionally high scholastic standing; his brilliance enabled him to skip three grades and enter Morehouse College in 1944, at the age of fifteen. After receiving a B.A. in sociology from Morehouse at nineteen, he followed in his father's footsteps and, in 1951, graduated with an "A" average from Crozier Theological Seminary in Chester, Pennsylvania with a Bachelor of Divinity degree.

King later became an ordained minister and, by 1955, completed his dissertation in philosophy and was awarded a Ph.D. from Boston University. In 1953, King's father officiated at his marriage to Corretta Scott. The couple later had four children, Yolanda Denise, Martin Luther III, Dexter Scott and Bernice Albertine. Dr. King was his father's assistant pastor at the Ebenezer Baptist Church, and eventually became the full-time pastor of Dexter Avenue Baptist Church in Montgomery, Alabama.

Dr. King's rise to national prominence began in December, 1955, in Montgomery, Alabama, when one tired Black woman, Rosa Parks, said; "No, I will not go to the back of the bus." For refusing to relinquish her seat to a White man, Mrs. Parks was jailed. Word of her arrest traveled all over Montgomery and within five days, the Montgomery Improvement Association (MIA) was organized with Dr. King as president. To bring about

---

a change in a long standing practice, King advised the people not to ride the Montgomery buses.

A boycott was organized and for over a year (381 days), Blacks picketed White businesses and refused to use public transportation. The cohesiveness of Blacks during this crisis resulted in a 1956 U.S. Supreme Court decision declaring Alabama's bus segregation laws unconstitutional. During the interim, King and his followers suffered undue harassment. King was arrested for staging an "illegal boycott."

When the boycott ended, King was among the first to board the newly desegregated buses. This victory established him as a prominent civil rights leader and spokesman for the masses of Black people. Shortly thereafter, with a group of southern ministers, King organized the Southern Christian Leadership Conferences (SCLU), in 1957, to further advance Black equality. Edward Nixon and Reverend Ralph Abernathy held high ranking positions in the SCLU organization.

Dr. King led nonviolent demonstrations for open housing, jobs and educational opportunities for Blacks across the nation. He also spoke out against the war in Vietnam. When King preached love for the oppressor, walking hand-in-hand with the poor and abused, people grew to love and respect him, and thousands flocked to him in support of the Black cause.

Realizing that the civil rights movement was behind them, college students united and started read-ins in public libraries, wade-ins in municipal swimming pools, eat-ins at lunch counters and stand-ins in movie houses. In 1960, it was reported that the NAACP spent 40% of its annual budget toward the defense of nearly 2,000 student protestors awaiting trial.

Although Dr. King walked in a Godly way and preached love for his fellow man, the blood of Black and White Americans once again soaked the flag of democracy. Civil rights leaders were assassinated systematically; college students were murdered and secretly buried; little children were victims of bombings in southern Black churches; peaceful demonstrators were harrassed by policemen with fire hoses; German shepherd dogs, trained to kill, were unleashed against the peaceful marchers. Dr. King, himself, was brutalized and arrested more than 30 times; his home was bombed, and his life and those of his family were threatened. He and sixteen other SCLC members were arrested for staging an eat-in in an exclusive restaurant, in St. Augustine, and were charged with violating Florida's "unwanted guest law."

On another occasion, King was sent to a Georgia State prison, which resulted in a national outcry from the American people. In times of crises, King never lost sight of his dream nor his commitment to nonviolence. "Let no man drag you so low as to hate," he would say. Along with a strong belief in the doctrine of Christianity, King held the teachings of nonviolence by Thoreau and Gandhi in high regard. He pleaded that Blacks should not seek to satisfy their thirst for freedom by drinking from the cup of bitterness and hatred.

In 1963, King and other Black leaders organized one of the greatest demonstrations in the history of the nation, "The March On Washington." He spoke to a crowd of over 250,000 people, dramatizing the shameful plight of Black Americans over the 100 years since the signing of the *Emancipation Proclamation*. Standing before the Lincoln Memorial, King gave his most eloquent "I Have a Dream" address, which touched the souls of every American. He stated that "100 years later, Blacks still are not free....Their lives are still crippled by the manacles of segregation and the chains of discrimination....Blacks live on a lonely island of poverty in the midst of a vast ocean of material prosperity." He further said, "Now is the time for America to make real her promise of democracy for all of her children."

In 1964, King watched President Lyndon B. Johnson sign a comprehensive *Civil Rights Bill,* which had been submitted previously by President John F. Kennedy. Dr. King's last demonstration was on March 28, 1968, when he led more than 6,000 protesters through downtown Memphis, Tennessee, in support of a sanitation workers' strike. On April 4, 1968, Dr King was assassinated as he stood talking with friends on the balcony of the Lorraine Motel in Memphis. He was survived by his wife, Coretta Scott King, four children, both parents, a sister and a brother. Funeral services at the Ebenezer Baptist Church in Atlanta were attended by thousands, including national and state officials, and entertainers.

For his outstanding contributions, Dr. Martin Luther King, Jr. received more than 300 honors and awards. In 1964, he and

Mrs. King traveled to Sweden and he received the world's highest honor—the Nobel Peace Prize. King kept the plaque, but donated the accompanying $54,000 to the SCLC for furthering the movement. *Time Magazine* named him "Man of the Year," and the NAACP awarded him the Spingarn Medal. *Stride Toward Freedom, Strength To Love,* and *Where Do We Go From Here* are a few of the books that King authored.

In 1968, Ras Al Khaima, an Arabian state, issued the first postage stamp in Dr. King's honor. Since that time, 22 countries have honored him with stamps, and the United States Postal Service has issued 166,435,000 commemorative stamps. In 1977, nine years after his death, the United States honored him with the nation's highest cilvilian award—the Medal of Freedom.

January, 1986, marked the beginning of the official national observance of Dr. King's birthday. Dr. Martin Luther King, Jr. left this comforting message with his people; "We as a people will get to the promised land."

MALCOLM X
1925-1965

Malcolm X, admired for his bare honesty, fiery personality and dramatic speeches, raised himself from the core of the Black ghetto and lashed out against the forces which perpetuated segregation, oppression and denial of Black worth. He did not believe in turning the other cheek; standing in direct opposition to the non-violent movement.

Malcolm X believed that it was a crime for any race to accept brutality without exercising means of self-defense. He stated, "If that's how Christian philosophy is interpreted, if that's what Gandhian philosophy teaches, well, then, I will call them criminal philosophies."

Malcolm X, born Malcolm Little on May 19, 1925 in Omaha, Nebraska, was the fourth of eight children of Earl and Louise Little. His father was a Baptist preacher who believed in the secular teachings of the nationalist Marcus Garvey. His mother was a mulatto born on the island of Grenada in the West Indies. White vigilantes ran the Littles out of Nebraska, and they settled in Lansing, Michigan, where Malcolm spent his early childhood. Klansmen burned the Littles' home and Mr. Little was beaten to death and left under the wheels of a streetcar. Although officials determined the death to be an accident, Malcolm felt it was caused by White racists. At the age of six, having no other avenue at his disposal to avenge his father's death, Malcolm began to hate all Whites.

Malcolm's mother moved the family to Detroit and they were separated. Ironically, Malcolm was placed in the foster care of a White couple who, by his own admission, treated him well. Although Malcolm possessed an above average intelligence and was an apt student, he dropped out of school after the eighth grade and ran away to Boston, and later to Harlem in New York. There, at age fifteen, he began a life of crime. "Detroit Red" or "Big Red," as he was called, melted into the underworld of numbers, drugs, confidence games, stealing, and prostitution. Before reaching his twenty-first birthday, he was sentenced to serve from eight to ten years in Massachusetts' state prison for burglary.

With prison came Malcolm's reform and a turning point in his life. He wisely used his prison time for self-education and scholarly development. In search of a cause to give meaning and worth to his life, he read avidly, including the entire contents of a Webster's dictionary. He learned of the Black Muslim movement and the teachings of Elijah Muhammad. When he re-entered society in 1952, he changed his name to Malcolm X and became an outstanding minister in the Nation of Islam.

In 1956, Malcolm's Harlem mosque was cited as one of the most successful. By the early 1960s, Malcolm was one of the most controversial and popular Black men in America, overshadowing his superior, Elijah Muhammad, so much that Malcolm was suspended from the ministry. Nevertheless, he continued to glorify Muhammad's name.

In 1963, Malcolm branched out on his own and formed the Organization of Afro-American Unity, becoming a hero in the eyes of many Black Americans. He traveled all over the States with a message of Black manhood and independence. Because Malcolm was a commanding and forceful speaker, he was also a busy lecturer at universities and a frequent guest on radio and television talk shows.

In 1964, Malcolm made a pilgrimage to Mecca, Saudi Arabia, and journeyed throughout Africa. The experience gained from these trips changed him greatly and he renounced Mr. Muhammad's teachings against all Whites. During a speech in New York City on February 21, 1965, Malcolm X was assassinated. Before his death, Malcolm X had overcome his hatred for Whites and had begun to realize that the races could work together to build a democratic society.

JOHN R. MITCHELL, JR.
1863-1929

John R. Mitchell, Jr., banker, politician, and a crusading Black journalist, spoke the truth without fear or concern for his personal welfare.

Born a slave in Richmond, Virginia, on July 11, 1863, to John and Rebecca Mitchell, young Mitchell worked as a carriage boy for James Lyons, a rich lawyer and a one-time owner of the Mitchell family. Often, when answering the doorbell, Mitchell would inform Mr. Lyons that a colored gentleman wished to see him. Lyons, a southern blue blood, tried to instill in young Mitchell that there was no such thing as a colored gentleman.

Lyons also opposed Mitchell's receiving an education, but, in spite of his protest, Mitchell's mother sent him to school. He graduated as valedictorian from high school in 1881. While in school, he won two gold medals: one for an oratorical contest, and another for his magnificent rendition of a map of the state of Virginia. Without the benefit of art lessons, his map, drawn in lead pencil, resembled the finest steel engraving.

Mitchell pursued a short-lived teaching career and, in 1884, took control of the *Richmond Planet*, a weekly newspaper. He was a bold and fearless writer, and under his leadership the journal became popular. His brave personal investigations of lynchings and murders occurring in the South, earned him the reputation of a vigorous and militant editor. Once a Black man was murdered by a White police officer, and a jury brought in a verdict that the man had died of an unknown disease. Mitchell discovered that the deceased had been unmercifully clubbed by the White officer. In his paper, he condemned the crime and declared the officer guilty of murder. For this,

Mitchell was summoned before a grand jury and an attempt was made to indict him.

On another occasion, which involved a lynching, Mitchell wrote in the *Richmond Planet* that the "murderers should be dangled from a rope's end." Two days later, he received an abusive letter from the lynchers, stating that "they would hang him, should he put his foot in their county." Mitchell replied in a followup editorial "there are no terrors in their threats because I am armed with honesty."

Around 1890, Blacks were being lynched on the flimsiest of pretexts. Mitchell advised his people to defend themselves. "The best remedy for a lyncher or a cursed midnight rider is a 16-shot Winchester rifle in the hands of a Black man who has nerve enough to pull the trigger," he wrote. As related by one historian, "his pen seemed dipped in vitriol (acid)."

At the time of the Spanish-American War, he strongly discouraged Blacks' participation, based on the facts that "a man who is not good enough to vote and hold office in a country is not good enough to fight and shed blood for it." The *New York World* said of him, "The fact that he is a Negro and lives in Richmond does not prevent him from being courageous almost to a fault." Mitchell won the presidency of the Afro-American Press Association and held that office from 1890 to 1894.

Up to the time of his death on December 3, 1929, John R. Mitchell continued to rally against racial injustices. He boycotted Richmond's segregated streetcars and lobbied against segregated neighborhoods. During WWI, postal officials confiscated the *Richmond Planet* because of articles written about the mistreatment of Black soldiers. It might be said that Mitchell went too far. Conversely, it might also be said, as one writer put it, "that he was the sort of man who would walk into the jaws of death to serve his race."

Isaac Myers, a businessman, Mason, and pioneer labor organizer, was founder and president of the first Black national labor union in American history.

Born on January 13, 1835 in Baltimore, Maryland, Isaac Myers was the only son of freeborn parents. Black children were deprived of educational opportunities, resulting in Myers being privately tutored by a local minister until his sixteenth birthday. He was later an apprentice to a well-known Black ship caulker. Myers became so proficient in his job that he was promoted to supervisor in one of the largest shipyards in Baltimore.

In Myers' time, the responsibility of caulkers was very important. The hulls of ships were made of wood and caulkers had the tedious job of applying pitch and gum to crevices between planks and beams to prevent leakage. Before the Civil War, Whites sought to drive Blacks out of the caulking trade by using violence. In 1865, White caulkers and ship carpenters joined forces to have Black caulkers and longshoremen discharged from the shipping trade in Baltimore. Supported by local government and police, they were successful.

Isaac Myers called a meeting of unemployed caulkers and took steps to counteract the removal of Blacks from the trade. He proposed that they form an all-Black union, called the Colored Caulker's Trade Union Society, by pooling their resources to purchase a shipyard and a railway. Stock was issued and Myers raised $10,000 from Blacks in Baltimore. He also borrowed $30,000 from a ship captain and took possession of the Chesapeake Marine Railway and Dry Dock Company in February of 1866.

Several months later, Myers hired more than 300 Black workers at an average wage of $3.00 per day. Under his supervision, his workers attained an outstanding reputation for excellent workmanship. Not only did Myers begin to receive contracts from White ship owners, but also from the United States government. In just five years, Myers was able to pay-off the $40,000 mortgage on his company and, as business expanded, added Whites to his list of employees.

Myers entertained the idea of organizing a Black labor union on a national scale, which would work cooperatively with White labor unions for the betterment of all union workers. His dream was realized when the White national labor union, in an unprecedented action, extended a formal invitation to all persons, regardless of color, to attend their annual convention. Myers attended the convention and was conmmissioned to investigate the prospect of organizing a national network. He succeeded, as a result of this involvement, in establishing the Colored National Labor Union in 1869, the first of its kind in American history.

Myers remained active in his local union, years after the demise of the CNLU. He held several government posts and was the owner of a coalyard. During his lifetime, he was organizer and president of the Maryland Colored State Industrial Fair Association; the Colored Businessmen's Association; the Colored Building and Loan Association; the Aged Ministers Home of the A.M.E. Church; and the superintendent of the Bethel A.M.E. School of Baltimore for fifteen years. He was also a grand master of the Maryland Masons and authored the *Mason's Digest.*

Isaac Myers died on January 28, 1891, and was survived by a second wife, Sarah, and his son George. His was the largest Black funeral, at that time, in Baltimore's history.

ASA PHILIP RANDOLPH
1889-1979

Asa Philip Randolph, a powerful union organizer and a civil rights leader, spent forty years of his life in constant battle for better working conditions and higher wages for all laborers. He founded the Brotherhood of Sleeping Car Porters, in 1925, and became its first president.

Asa Randolph, born on April 15, 1889, in Crescent City, Florida, was the son of Jaynes W. Randolph, an itinerant minister of slave parentage who belonged to a Virginia plantation owner named John Randolph. After completing high school, Asa traveled to New York City and entered City College.

Randolph fancied himself a writer, and with a friend, founded a journal, *The Messenger*. It was an outspoken, highly opinionated, radical magazine which did not gain financial success. However, it did serve as a vehicle for Randolph's viewpoints on war and capitalism. His views as a socialist was that a decent, well-paying job was the first step towards social and political freedom. He saw the condition of American Blacks and other minorities as the symptom of a larger social illness caused by an unfair distribution of power, wealth and resources.

By 1925, the Pullman Company, builders/operators of sleeping cars and parlor cars for the nation's railroads, was the largest single employer of Blacks in the United States. It paid its 12,000 porters about $60.00 per month for 400 hours or 11,000 miles, whichever came first. Porters were required to pay for their meals and to purchase their own uniforms and equipment. They were not compensated for the five hours of preparation time before or any overtime. They also worked straight through without layover time.

Randolph was secretly asked to organize the porters because he was an outsider and could not be hurt by the Pullman Company. After several meetings, the Brotherhood of Sleeping

Car Porters was formed on August 25, 1925. The Pullman Company did everything in its power to stop the union. The organization was in constant battle for twelve years, but the Pullman Company finally conceded to their demands. Twelve years to the day, August 25, 1937, Pullman's president announced to the Brotherhood negotiators, "Gentlemen, the Pullman Company is ready to sign." History was made. It was the first time a contract had been signed between a Black union and an American corporation.

This union contract included a wage settlement of $1.25 million, and the porters' work month was reduced from 400 hours to 240 hours. The victory placed Randolph in the upper echelon of Black leadership. Later, Randolph's Brotherhood joined the American Federation of Labor (AFL). When the AFL merged with the Congress of Industrial Organizations (CIO) in 1955, Randolph was named vice-president of the AFL-CIO Executive Council becoming the highest ranking Black in the trade union movement.

Also, between 1940 and 1948, Randolph was highly instrumental in desegregating the war industries, federal employment, and the armed forces. In 1963, he was responsible for organizing and bringing together over 250,000 people, of all races, in the historic "March on Washington" for jobs and freedom. It was at this gathering that Dr. Martin Luther King, Jr. gave his famous "I Have a Dream" address, which stirred the souls of the nation.

The greatness of Asa Philip Randolph and his contributions to Black Americans can never be forgotten, for they are recorded in the pages of history and remembered in the hearts of men. Randolph died, at age ninety, in 1979.

JOSEPHINE ST. PIERRE RUFFIN
1842-1924

Josephine Ruffin gained national prominence as a civic leader and an organizer of Black women's clubs. Founder of the well-known New Era Club of Boston, she was also instrumental in publishing the first Black women's newspaper in the United States.

Josephine Ruffin, born in Boston on August 31, 1842, was the sixth child of John and Eliza St. Pierre. Both parents were of mixed ancestry: French, English, Indian and African royalty. Her mother was born in Cornwall, England, and her father was a clothes merchant and founder of Zion Baptist Church in Boston.

According to family records, her paternal grandfather was an African Prince, who escaped from a slave ship near an Indian settlement. Because schools were segregated in Boston up to 1855, her parents sent her to school in Salem, Massachusetts. She later continued her education in Boston until she married the prestigious George L. Ruffin, at the tender age of sixteen.

Hoping to escape racial discrimination, the couple lived in Liverpool, England until the start of the Civil War. Returning to the States, they became fighters in the struggle for Black equality. Mr. Ruffin worked as a barber while attending Harvard University and later became a state legislator, a city council member, and Boston's first Black municipal judge. The couple parented five children, all of whom became successful.

Josephine Ruffin gained social acceptance and directed her efforts in promoting Black causes. Busying herself with local welfare needs and the women's suffrage movement, she helped organize, in 1879, the Boston Kansas Relief Association, which provided money, clothing and food to the masses of Blacks relocating to Kansas. She was a charter member of the Association Charities of Boston, and an executive board member of the Massachusetts Moral Education Association.

Although Josephine Ruffin is remembered for her struggle for the advancement of Blacks in general, her main concern was the elevation of Black women in particular. In 1894, she started the Women's New Era Club and edited its monthly newspaper, *Women's Era*. Within one year, she called in other clubs which led to the organization of the National Federation of Afro-American Women. It's aim was to demonstrate the existence of a large growing class of intelligent, cultured Black women, and to refute public charges of ignorance and immorality.

In 1896, the NFAAW merged with a rival organization, headed by the famed Mary Church Terrell, to become the National Association of Colored Women. In the same year, Ruffin was also instrumental in the formation of the Northeastern Federation of Women's Clubs.

Josephine Ruffin became a member of the New England Women's Press Association and an executive board member of both the Massachusetts State Federation of Women's Clubs and the General Federation of Women's Clubs.

In 1900, as a delegate of one Black and two White clubs, she attended the National Convention of Women's Clubs in Wisconsin. Highly insulted when opposed by southern White women (the board refused to ratify the acceptance of the Black New Era club), Ruffin emphatically refused to represent the White clubs because they denied membership to the Black club.

Years later, the New Era Club faded into oblivion, but Ruffin remained active for the betterment of Blacks. She founded the Association for the Promotion of Child Training in the South, and was active in the NAACP. In 1902, she founded the American Mount Coffee School Association to raise funds to enlarge the association's school in Liberia. She served as the school's vice-president. Josephine Ruffin died of nephritis in 1924, at the age of eighty-one.

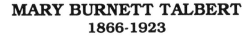

MARY BURNETT TALBERT
1866-1923

Mary Burnett Talbert, an educator, Red Cross nurse during WWI, staunch civil rights advocate, founder of the Christian Culture Congress, president of the National Association of Colored Women, director of the NAACP, and a true trailblazer.

Mary was born in Oberlin, Ohio, in 1866, and attended Oberlin public schools. Mary, the only Black student in her class at Oberlin College, received her Bachelor's degree, at age nineteen in 1886. After graduation, she accepted the position of assistant principal of Bethel University in Little Rock, Arkansas. In 1887, she resigned this post to become the principal of Little Rock's Union High School, and was the first Black in the history of Arkansas to hold such a high post. Later she met and married William A. Talbert.

The Talberts relocated to Buffalo, New York, where she lived for the rest of her life. Apparently, she continued her education in Buffalo; some historians credit her with earning a Ph.D. from Buffalo University at an unspecified date. She became involved in social services. While treasurer of the Michigan Avenue Baptist Church, she founded the Christian Culture Congress, giving twenty years of service as its president.

Talbert was a charter member of New York State's Federation of Colored Women, and later held the position of president. From 1916 to 1921, she was president of the National Association of Colored Women (NACW). While holding this office, she presided over the committee responsible for restoring the celebrated Frederick Douglas home in Anacostia, D.C. In 1920, she represented the NACW as an international delegate at the sixth quinquennial meeting of the International Council of Women in Christiania, Norway.

During World War I, Mrs. Talbert served her country by assisting the War Loan Department. She personally solicited the purchase of thousands of dollars in Liberty Bonds. She also enlisted as a Red Cross nurse and saw active duty in France with the American Expeditionary Forces. To the men bound for the battlefront, her services were invaluable; she provided comfort and religious training, which uplifted the spirits of American men facing death on foreign soil.

After the war, Mrs. Talbert returned to the States and directed her attention to the war on racial prejudices and discrimination. As vice-president and director of the NAACP, she championed prison reforms in southern states. As chairman of the Anti-Lynching Crusaders, she traveled thousands of miles all over the United States, urging Blacks and Whites alike to support the passage of the *Dyer Anti-Lynching Bill.*

Unfortunately, the Bill never passed the Senate, however, it did expose the shameful way in which Blacks were brutalized and murdered unjustly during this era. In Talbert's crusade, she raised $12,000. She also traveled extensively in Europe, lecturing on race relations, women's rights, and the overall plight of the Black race in America.

In 1922, Mary Burnett Talbert was the first Black woman to receive the prestigious NAACP Spingarn Award, the highest honor awarded to Blacks. She died a year later in 1923.

CHANNING H. TOBIAS
1882-1961

Channing H. Tobias, an outstanding religious and civic leader, and a prominent YMCA official, played an active role in advocating interracial cooperation during the thirties and forties.

Channing Tobias was born on February 1, 1882, in Augusta, Georgia. His father worked as a coachman, and his mother, who died when he was twelve, was a domestic servant.

After receiving an early education at Haines Institute, a B.A. from Paine Institute in 1902, and a B.S. from Drew University in 1905. He taught biblical subjects at Paine from 1905 to 1911. Later, he began a long and outstanding association with the YMCA. Tobias married Mary Pritchard in 1908, and they had two daughters. Mary died in 1949, and he married Eva Gassett Arnold in 1951.

For twelve years, Tobias served as secretary of the National Council of the YMCA, in charge of the International Committee. From 1923 to 1946, he was senior secretary of the Colored Department of the National Council. He used the Christian doctrine as a basis for promoting race relations. In 1946, he became the first Black director of the Phelps-Stokes Fund, an organization that provided educational opportunities to Blacks.

In addition, Tobias served on the board of directors of the Marshall Field and Jessie Smith Noyes Foundations, the Stettinius Associates of Liberia, and the American Bible Society. He was elected to the board of trustees of the NAACP and later became chairman of the board, holding this office until his retirement in 1959. Beyond these major responsibilities, Tobias held significant government posts and traveled all over the world.

Tobias attended the Second Pan-African Congress in Paris, in 1921, was a delegate and speaker at the World Conference of the YMCA, at Helsingfors, Finland in 1926. While abroad, he lectured in Poland and Czechoslovakia. Tobias was one of two Blacks, among a twelve-party U.S. delegation, to attend a World Conference of the YMCA in Mysore, India in 1936; and he later attended another YMCA Conference in Denmark, in 1950.

Tobias was a member of the Joint Army and Navy Committee on Welfare and Recreation during WWII; the National Advisory Committee on Selective Service; the Civilian Committee of the U.S. Navy in 1946; President Truman's Committee on Civil Rights (1946-47); and the Mayor's Committee on Survey Management of New York City. During 1951-52, as an alternate U.S. special assignment delegate to the sixth General Assembly of the United Nations in Paris, his travels took him to the Near East, Africa and the Far East.

Tobias' uncanny ability to calm ruffled waters between the races established him as an effective race-relations specialist. In 1944, he attacked segregation in Protestant churches, schools, and all forms of public transportation. He denounced the Red Cross and its preferential treatment in the distribution of blood plasma, the maltreatment of Black nurses, and the denial of equal opportunity for employment by industry and organized labor. At the World Conference of the YMCA in India, he did not falter in stating, "America and South Africa are practically the only countries in the world where racial exclusion is practiced within the YMCA."

Channing Tobias died on November 5, 1961, after a long illness. Among the many honors he received are the Harmon Award for Religious Services, the NAACP Spingarn Award for Distinguished Achievement, an honorary D.D. from Gammon Theological Seminary, and an LL.D. from Morehouse College. He was also, the first Black to receive an honorary LL.D. from the University of New York.

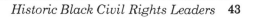

WALTER FRANCIS WHITE
1896-1955

Walter Francis White fought strongly for equality in voting rights, challenged segregation and discrimination in education and travel, and also drew national attention to the evil of lynchings. He was a noted author, legal advisor and special investigator for the NAACP.

Walter was born on July 1, 1896, in Atlanta, Georgia, to George and Madeline White. He and his father were fair skinned, blue-eyed and could "pass" for White men. When Walter was thirteen, during the Atlanta race riots, his home was the target of a bloodthirsty, White racist mob. Anticipating the worst on one particular night, he and his father waited inside their home all night with guns drawn. Walter later recalled, "I discovered what it meant to be a Negro." He also bitterly remembered that his father died in a Georgia hospital, while White doctors argued over whether the patient was Black or White.

After graduating from Atlanta University in 1916, Walter became active in the Black community. When the board of education sought to end education for Blacks after the sixth grade, he organized a campaign and fought the board's decision. This incident led to the organization of a local branch of the NAACP with Walter as secretary. The school board was later forced to change its policy.

In 1918, White was invited to join the New York NAACP staff, as assistant secretary, and quickly proved himself invaluable. In 1920, James Weldon Johnson became the first Black national secretary of the NAACP and, for the next decade, he and Walter ran the organization successfully. Walter Francis White was aggressive, quick witted, and proved to be an administrator *par excellence*. Although he was not a lawyer, he was able to master complex legal matters and acted as admmistrator for the NAACP's legal committee.

As part of his aggressive campaign against mob violence, White volunteered to undertake the dangerous job of investigating some of the most shocking lynchings. He risked his life to gather evidence on behalf of the rights of Blacks. Because he was of fair complexion, he was able to infiltrate mob meetings and secure valuable information. On one such occasion in Arkansas, he barely escaped being hanged. In 1931, he succeeded Johnson as national secretary of the NAACP. And, throughout White's administration, the NAACP remained committed in fighting for the enforcement of Blacks' constitutional rights.

In addition to his involvement in the NAACP, White was a delegate to the Second Pan African Congress, held in Europe in 1921, and a consultant to the U.S. delegation at the San Francisco Conference, which organized the United Nations in 1945. As a war correspondent for the *New York Post,* he wrote first hand reports about the European, Mediterranean, Middle East, and Pacific war zones.

White also participated in the Round-the-World Town Meeting of the Air; visiting Egypt, India, Israel, Japan and the Caribbean. He wrote articles for more than a dozen prestigious journals and authored six popular books: *The Fire in the Flint, Flight, Rope and Faggot; A Rising Wind; A Man Called White;* and *How Far the Promised Land.* He was awarded the Spingarn Medal from the NAACP, and the Guggenheim Fellowship Award for his first two novels.

Walter F. White died of a heart attack, in 1955, and was survived by a wife and two children. A strategist and builder of the NAACP, he made the organization a major force in American society.

WHITNEY MOORE YOUNG, JR.
1921-1971

Although the civil rights movement strove to open doors of opportunity for Blacks, under Whitney M. Young's leadership, the Urban League equipped Blacks to actually walk through those doors. Young was the Executive Director of the National Urban League.

Born on July 31, 1921, in Lincoln Ridge, Kentucky, the only child of Whitney and Laura Ray Young, Whitney graduated from Lincoln Institute, at age fourteen, with an "A" average and entered Kentucky State College, graduating in 1941. In 1947, he received an M.A. in social work from the University of Minnesota. In 1954, he was appointed Dean of Atlanta University's College of Social Work. He also served as Vice-President of the NAACP in Georgia. Later, he married Margaret Buckner, and enlisted in the Army during WWII.

In 1961, the Urban League sought a new director and Young was approached. He accepted the position in August. His arrival was likened to a fresh breeze. He restructured the national headquarters, expanded the scope of programs, and developed new projects to improve employment opportunities. He developed the National Skills Bank, which sought to place the unemployed and underemployed in marketable positions, which utilized their talents.

These on-the-job training programs placed unskilled workers in training positions in private industry, while the Broadcast Skills Bank found jobs for Blacks in radio and television. During the first seven years of Young's leadership, on-the-job training produced 50,000 workers, and the League reported up to 50,000 placements annually in new or upgraded jobs.

Not only did Young expand the services of the League, but the organization itself grew from sixty-three affiliates to ninety-eight. The professional staff increased from 300 to over 1,200, and its income grew from $340,000, in 1961, to $14,749,000 by 1970. Because of his belief in Young, McGeorge Bundy, president of the Ford Foundation, gave the League $6,630,000 (from 1966-1969) for its general support, and for the establishment of a fair housing project. Henry Ford II gave the Urban League a yearly check of $100,000.

As the civil rights movement advanced, Young broke from the usual stance of the Urban League's sideline observance and sought to bridge the gap between the movement and the League. He argued that by communicating with the people, the League would be in a better position to advise contributors on matters regarding Blacks. In 1963, Young made a concerted effort to establish a dialogue with prominent civil rights leaders. As a result, the Council for United Civil Rights Leadership was organized.

While the Urban League did not actually participate in demonstrations, it lent moral support, mediated, conducted fact finding surveys, and negotiated grievances between the demonstrators and the power structure. At the 1963 "March on Washington," the League's stance became public knowledge. Young clearly stated in his speech, "Although each organization has its own unique role to fulfill within the movement, we are all united as never before on the goal of securing first class citizenship for all Americans—now!"

Throughout his life, Whitney Young continued to fight for Black Americans. Over the years, he served on nearly a dozen presidential panels, was a founding member of the Urban Coalition, served on the boards of the Rockefeller Foundation, Urban American, Inc., and the New York Federal Reserve Bank. He also authored two books, *To Be Equal*, and *Beyond Racisim*.

Whitney Moore Young drowned in a swimming accident in Lagos, Nigeria in March of 1971. He was survived by his wife, Margaret, and two daughters, Marcie and Laureen. While others led protests and walked on picket lines, Young marched his people to job training centers, better housing and educational institutions.

I Have A Dream
(Excerpt)

I say to you today, my friends, that in spite of the difficulties and frustrations of the moment I still have a dream. It is a dream deeply rooted in the American dream.

I have a dream that one day this nation will rise up and live out the true meaning of its creed: "We hold these truths to be self-evident; that all men are created equal."

I have a dream that one day on the red hills of Georgia the sons of former slaves and the sons of former slaveowners will be able to sit down together at the table of brotherhood.

I have a dream that one day even the state of Mississippi, a desert state sweltering with the heat of injustice and oppression, will be transformed into an oasis of freedom and justice.

I have a dream that one day my four little children will one day live in a nation where they will not be judged by the color of their skin but by the content of their character.

I have a dream today.

I have a dream that one day the state of Alabama, whose governor's lips are presently dripping with the words of interposition and nullification, will be trans formed into a situation where little black boys and black girls will be able to join hands with little white boys and white girls and walk together as sisters and brothers.

I have a dream today.

I have a dream that every valley shall be exalted, every hill and mountain shall be made low, the rough places will be made plains, and the crooked places will be made straight, and the glory of the Lord shall be revealed, and all flesh shall see it together.

This is our hope. This is the faith with which I return to the South. With this faith we will be able to transform the jangling discords of our nation into a beautiful symphony of brotherhood. With this faith we will be able to work together, to pray together, to struggle together, to go to jail together, to stand up for freedom together, knowing that we will be free one day.

This will be the day when all of God's children will be able to sing with new meaning "My country 'tis of thee, sweet land of liberty, of thee I sing. Land where my fathers died, land of the pilgrim's pride, from every mountainside, let freedom ring."

And if America is to be a great nation this must become true. So let freedom ring from the prodigious hilltops of New Hampshire. Let freedom ring from the mighty mountains of New York. Let freedom ring from the heightening Alleghenies of Pennsylvania!

Let freedom ring from the snowcapped Rockies of Colorado!

Let freedom ring from the curvaceous peaks of California!

But not only that; let freedom ring from the Stone Mountain of Georgia!

Let freedom ring from every hill and molehill of Mississippi. From every mountainside, let freedom ring.

When we let freedom ring, when we let it ring from every village and every hamlet, from every state and every city, we will be able to speed up that day when all of God's children, black men and white men, Jews and Gentiles, Protestants and Catholics, will be able to join hands and sing in the words of that old Negro spiritual, "Free at last! Free at last! Thank God almighty, we are free at last! "

Martin Luther King, Jr.
Washington, D.C.
August 28, 1963

TEST YOURSELF

Now that you have familiarized yourself with our historic Black Civil Rights Leaders, in this fourth series of Empak's Black History publications, this section, in three parts: MATCH; TRUE/FALSE; MULTIPLE CHOICE/FILL-IN, is designed to help you remember some key points about each notable Black Civil Rights Leader. (Answers on page 28)

MATCH

I. *Match the column on the right with the column on the left by placing the appropriate alphabetical letter next to the civil rights leader it represents.*

1. W.E.B. DuBois _____   A) "Let no man drag you so low as to hate"
2. George Downing _____   B) "Unregistered foreign agent"
3. Fannie Hamer _____   C) "Gentlemen, we're ready to sign"
4. Dr. Martin Luther King, Jr. _____   D) "There is no terror in your threats."
5. John Mitchell _____   E) "I didn't register for you. . . ."
6. Asa Randolph _____   F) "Calmed ruffled waters"
7. Channing Tobias _____   G) "Send me anyone who may complain."

TRUE/FALSE

II. *The True and False statements below are taken from the biographical information given on each of the leaders.*

1. Whitney Young headed the National YMCA Council. _____
2. Josephine Ruffin is noted for organizing women's clubs. _____
3. Dr. George Haynes founded the National Urban League. _____
4. James Farmer was the first Black man to run for United States president. _____
5. Marcus Garvey was the founder of the Universal Negro Industrial Association. _____
6. Jesse Jackson, the founder of Operation PUSH, also founded CORE in 1942. _____
7. Malcolm X believed in non-violent tactics and was always willing to turn the other cheek. _____

MULTIPLE CHOICE/FILL-IN

III. *Complete the statements below by drawing a line under the correct name, or by filling-in the correct answer which you have read in the biographical sketches.*

1. _____ organized the Brotherhood of Sleeping Car Porters in 1925.
2. (Daisy Bates, Fannie Lou Hamer) earned the title "First Lady of Civil Rights."
3. In 1945, _____ was a consultant to the U.S. delegation which organized the United Nations.
4. In 1922, _____ was the first Black woman to receive the NAACP's Spingarn Medal for its highest achievement.
5. _____ founded the MIA, SCLC and was awarded the highest honors in this nation and in the world.
6. This Presbyterian minister (James Farmer, George Haynes, Francis Grimké) attacked racism from his pulpit. He openly critized the American Bible Society and noted White evangelists.
7. (John Mitchell, Isaac Myers, W.E.B. DuBois) was the founder and president of the first Black national labor union in America.
8. Listed in *Who's Who Among American Women*, _____ was "One of the Top Nine News Personalities of the World in 1957."

49

CROSSWORD PUZZLE

ACROSS

2. Railway and Dry Dock
4. Descendant from African royalty
6. Gandhi disciple
8. Up! You mighty race!
9. The absence of color
10. Tough kid on the block
12. Fire and brimstone
14. Civil servant
15. "Then, there were nine"
16. "I am...."
17. Cultivator
18. Acid pen
19. American radical

DOWN

1. Detroit Red
3. On-the-Job Training
5. Not ready in Mississippi
7. Angel of mercy
11. Urban affairs
13. AFL-CIO

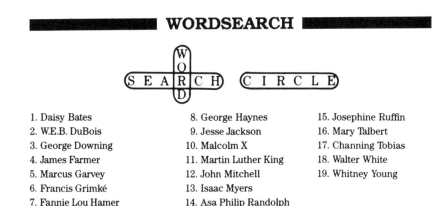

1. Daisy Bates
2. W.E.B. DuBois
3. George Downing
4. James Farmer
5. Marcus Garvey
6. Francis Grimké
7. Fannie Lou Hamer
8. George Haynes
9. Jesse Jackson
10. Malcolm X
11. Martin Luther King
12. John Mitchell
13. Isaac Myers
14. Asa Philip Randolph
15. Josephine Ruffin
16. Mary Talbert
17. Channing Tobias
18. Walter White
19. Whitney Young

The names of our nineteen HISTORIC BLACK CIVIL RIGHTS LEADERS are contained in the diagram below. Look in the diagram of letters for the names given in the list. Find the names by reading FORWARD, BACKWARDS, UP, DOWN, and DIAGONALLY in a straight line of letters. Each time you find a name in the diagram, circle it in the diagram and cross it off on the list of names. Words often overlap, and letters may be used more than once.

```
N E M M H G N I N W O D E G R O E G T L M C N W B C T
O S A E A I J S O P K L A O B X Y D H A R H M W C E Z
S I R P Q L O D R I E S T K W J M S R L S T V H D V A
K B Y E S T C A W R I N T H E W O C R L D R O I B A C
C I T I D Y J O A L K J E V O L U A C M Y E A T J N F
A B A L A C K H L I A S T O R S Y K I T S M P N E S I
J E L P M O D E T M E R F E G A S D J Y K A O E S C G
E O B A W A L T E S X C M A W G E O R G E H A Y N E S
S N E G E A O S R F A H R D N R H I R Y T U K Y A F A
S A R B N C F K W D T V E I F N C E G L S O N O B H I
E H T R I A I J H O E L K M M H E N I I G L E U O B B
J G U B R N S W I Y P R Q I N N R V O S T E E N R L O
U O V M G W E P T X E Y T Z W A I B M O B I R G S L T
J B E F A C C D E H E C F G O C U H S V P N G H I O G
C R A K N A L I I T M H J E S R D N O W A R N C I V R N
P R O A C R G U S E T U O S B O R N E V W A X Y I R I
M Z D A D N L E L F J O S E P H I N E R U F F I N A N
J O L E A N G L M A R G W E N T A L L E Y O H N C C N
H I J K I S A A C M Y E R S L S G N I H C N Y L E I A
M N O T Z C R H P L O D N A R P I L I H P A S A S T H
B A R C I Z S E H L K V O D E A P D O L S R V A C T C
D A I S Y B A T E S C R A Z I V E Y J O V S T L Z O A
M K C M Q P L D S R R F R A N C I S G R I M K E S D C
```

51

MATCH

1.–B	5.–D
2.–G	6.–C
3.–E	7.–F
4.–A	

TRUE/FALSE

1.–FALSE	5.–TRUE
2.–TRUE	6.–FALSE
3.–TRUE	7.–FALSE
4.–FALSE	

MULTIPLE CHOICE

1.–ASA RANDOLPH	5.–MARTIN LUTHER KING, JR.
2.–FANNIE LOU HAMER	6.–FRANCIS GRIMKE
3.–WALTER WHITE	7.–ISAAC MYERS
4.–MARY TALBERT	8.–DAISY BATES

CROSSWORD PUZZLE   WORDSEARCH

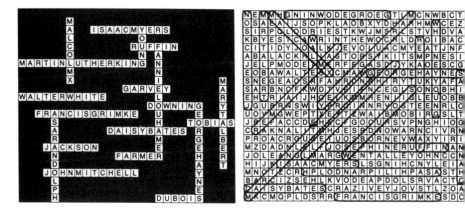

Name _____

Affiliation _____

Address _____
P. O. Box numbers not accepted, street address must appear.

City _____ **State** _____ **Zip** _____

Phone# (_____)_____ Date _____

Method Of Payment Enclosed:　( ) Check　　　( ) Money Order　　　( ) Purchase Order

Prices effective 11/1/95 thru 10/31/96

ADVANCED LEVEL

Quantity	ISBN #	Title Description	Unit Price	Total Price
	0-922162-1-8	"A Salute to Historic Black Women"		
	0-922162-2-6	"A Salute to Black Scientists & Inventors"		
	0-922162-3-4	"A Salute to Black Pioneers"		
	0-922162-4-2	"A Salute to Black Civil Rights Leaders"		
	0-922162-5-0	"A Salute to Historic Black Abolitionists"		
	0-922162-6-9	"A Salute to Historic African Kings & Queens"		
	0-922162-7-7	"A Salute to Historic Black Firsts"		
	0-922162-8-5	"A Salute to Historic Blacks in the Arts"		
	0-922162-9-3	"A Salute to Blacks in the Federal Government"		
	0-922162-14-X	"A Salute to Historic Black Educators"		

INTERMEDIATE LEVEL

Quantity	ISBN #	Title Description	Unit Price	Total Price
	0-922162-75-1	"Historic Black Women"		
	0-922162-76-X	"Black Scientists & Inventors"		
	0-922162-77-8	"Historic Black Pioneers"		
	0-922162-78-6	"Black Civil Rights Leaders"		
	0-922162-80-8	"Historic Black Abolitionists"		
	0-922162-81-6	"Historic African Kings & Queens"		
	0-922162-82-4	"Historic Black Firsts"		
	0-922162-83-2	"Historic Blacks in the Arts"		
	0-922162-84-0	"Blacks in the Federal Government"		
	0-922162-85-9	"Historic Black Educators"		

Total Books			❸ Subtotal	
			❹ IL Residents add 8.75% Sales Tax	
		SEE ABOVE CHART ▷	❺ Shipping & Handling	
GRADE LEVEL: 4th, 5th, 6th			❻ Total	

BOOK PRICING ● QUANTITY DISCOUNTS

Advanced Level	Intermediate Level
Reg. $3.49	Reg. $2.29
Order 50 or More	Order 50 or More
Save 40¢ EACH	Save 20¢ EACH
@ $3.09	@ $2.09

❺ SHIPPING AND HANDLING

Order Total	Add
Under $5.00	$1.50
$5.01-$15.00	$3.00
$15.01-$35.00	$4.50
$35.01-$75.00	$7.00
$75.01-$200.00	10%
Over $201.00	6%

In addition to the above charges, U.S. territories, HI & AK, add $2.00. Canada & Mexico, add $5.00. Other outside U.S., add $20.00.

Name _____

Affiliation _____

Street _____
P. O. Box numbers not accepted, street address must appear.

City _____ State _____ Zip _____

Phone (_____)_____ Date _____

Method Of Payment Enclosed:　　( ) Check　　　　( ) Money Order　　　　( ) Purchase Order

Prices effective 11/1/95 thru 10/31/96

PRIMARY LEVEL... KINDERGARTEN, FIRST, SECOND & THIRD GRADE

Quantity	ISBN #	Title Description	Unit Price	Total Price
	0-922162-90-5	"Kumi and Chanti"		
	0-922162-91-3	"George Washington Carver"		
	0-922162-92-1	"Harriet Tubman"		
	0-922162-93-X	"Jean Baptist DuSable"		
	0-922162-94-8	"Matthew Henson"		
	0-922162-95-6	"Bessie Coleman"		
	Total Books		❸ Subtotal	
			❹ IL Residents add 8.75% Sales Tax	
	SEE CHART BELOW ▷		❺ Shipping & Handling	
			❻ Total	

KEY STEPS IN ORDERING

❶ Establish quantity needs.　　❹ Add tax, if applicable.
❷ Determine book unit price.　　❺ Add shipping &handling.
❸ Determine total cost.　　❻ Total amount.

BOOK PRICING ● QUANTITY DISCOUNTS

❶ Quantity Ordered	❷ Unit Price
1-49	$3.49
50 +	$3.09

❺ SHIPPING AND HANDLING

Order Total	Add
Under $5	$1.50
$5.01-$15.00	$3.00
$15.01- $35.00	$4.50
$35.01-$75.00	$7.00
$75.01-$200.00	10%
Over $201.00	6%

In addition to the above charges, U.S. territories, HI & AK, add $2.00. Canada and Mexico, add $5.00. Other outside U.S., add $20.00.

Empak Publishing provides attractive counter and floor displays for retailers and organizations interested in the Heritage book series for resale. Please check here ☐ and include this form with your letterhead and we will send you specific information and our special volume discounts.

- The Empak "Heritage Kids" series provides a basic understanding and appreciation of Black history which translates to cultural awareness, self-esteem, and ethnic pride within young African-American children.

- Assisted by dynamic and impressive 4-color illustrations, readers will be able to relate to the two adorable African kids -- Kumi & Chanti, as they are introduced to the inspirational lives and deeds of significant, historic African-Americans.

Black History Materials
Available from Empak Publishing

A Salute To Black History Poster Series
African-American Experience–Period Poster Series
Biographical Poster Series
Heritage Kids Poster Series

Advanced Booklet Series
Instructor's Manuals
Advanced Skills Sheets
Black History Bulletin Board Aids
Instructor's Kits

Intermediate Booklet Series
Teacher's Guides
Intermediate Skill Sheets
Black History Flashcards
Intermediate Reading Certificates
Teacher's Kits

Heritage Kids Booklet Series
Heritage Kids Resource & Activity Guides
Heritage Kids Reading Certificates
Heritage Kids Kits

Black History Videos
Black History Month Activity & Resource Guide
African-American Times–A Chronological Record
African-American Discovery Board Game
African-American Clip Art
Black History Mugs
Black Heritage Marble Engraving
Black History Month Banners (18" x 60")
Say YES to Black History Education Sweatshirts
Say YES to Black History Education T-Shirts

To receive your copy of the Empak Publishing Company's
colorful new catalog, please send $2 to cover postage and handling to:

Empak Publishing Company
Catalog Dept., Suite 300
212 East Ohio Street
Chicago, IL 60611